I0713288

Yendor D. Wolf

**Haiku Writer
And Martial Artist
Extraordinaire**

Presents

The Wolf's Travels

Volume 2:
The Five Wolves

Dedication

Born into the world
Gently striding on life's path
Alone, Together

This book is dedicated to
the school, the home, of Wolf Style.

May all past and future practitioners exemplify
the Way of Survival.

Editor's Note

In all my years of editing and writing, there's one thing I always believed: Experience is greater than formal education. Where does this idea come from? Life! And reading hundreds of works from hoity-toity MFAs and PhDs filled with pretentious hogwash.

Of all the writers I've had the pleasure of working with, Yendor was one of the few who could back up his haikus with his fists: a deadly combo.

This magazine erupted with nothing but a binder full of writings, $400, and an allergy to pretension, haughtiness, and pocket squares. The only way I got my writing out was to speed through with acid and grit.

One fateful day, Yendor came to the 5/7/5 Magazine offices seeking a career. I could tell this man wasn't one to shy away from a good story. His work, the epitome of a chef's kiss. Fighters' sweat sprang from the pages, the smell of the blood wafted my nostrils. I was itching for a fight just reading it. You'd expect a violent figure to conjure up such pieces, yet what stood in front of me was a polite young man with an endearing smile wanting to fulfill his dream.

He traveled the nation recording encounters, thoughts, and feelings, defended his World's Strongest Fighter title in the World Adult Fighting League (WAFL), and yet had the humility to pass on his knowledge to us common folks. I just had to get his work to the public.

Wolf Style, a fascinating physical art form that imbues the practitioner with beyond-expert grappling ability, tremendous stamina, and the will to endure all of life's hardships. You won't get a buff body reading haikus, but you'll get an education in recognizing your self-worth.

Now, stop reading my note, sink your teeth into this book, and start discovering your way of life.

From the desk of

ROY F. PATRICKSON,

EDITOR-IN-CHIEF

A Note on Style

First and foremost, Wolf Style deals with meditation on the Self; how one survives within the world depends on their mindset and actions.

Secondly, there is no apprehension about death or pain. This is crucial to the survival of the body and spirit.

As one progresses toward themselves, meditations on death will become the norm.

Further, contemplate any knowledge gained throughout this book and do not enforce what you've learned as the Only Way. Share it, interrogate it, and sculpt it to become your way of life.

Finally, do not focus on one tenet over others. This will hobble a fighter, preventing usefulness.

Message from the Author

Wow, another book. How lucky am I to share this volume with you—a book near and dear to me as it introduces the tenets of my style, Wolf Style of Combat (Kombat de Lou).

I attended the martial arts school in Haiti when I was five, and exited 14 years later as a Master of all Wolf forms. That episode of my life was the start of a new journey of self-discovery. Over the years, I meditated on the principles of the martial art and made a few discoveries, which I am humbled to share in this volume, along with stories of the other wolves, who are my greatest friends.

Please take this book and the haikus within as a thoughtful respite on your own journey toward self-discovery.

Thank you.

THE
GREY
CHAPTER

LUKE
OLD GREY WOLF
FERDINAND

Age: 86

Favorite Food: PB&J sandwiches

Background: Introduced to the Wolf style after 35 years of Aikido, Judo, and Tai Chi training. At 55, he mastered the first phase of the style. Always a beginner in a constant state of conscious realization.

Ten years ago, we ran warmup drills in the morning: 1 minute of jumping jacks, 1 minute of spider crawls, 3 30-second bridge poses, 10-meter gorilla hop, 30-second hip circles (both directions), pushups for 30 seconds, and finally neck bridges, 15 front and back. While reliving the basics, I noticed Old Grey slowing halfway through each one. He finished, but as he's the oldest Wolf in our group, I harbored some concern for his health, even as we all hurdled towards our own limits. But on this day, it was just us. Before starting drills, I asked if he needed time to rest. He cocked an eyebrow and a guffaw burst from his belly, out through his throat.

"I've wondered that, too. As if y'all racing for the warm-up trophy." He started stretching his calves. "Yeah, I'm old, but me slowing down is to help me find my trouble areas. Like today, the gorilla hops reminded me that my knees need a bit of loosening up, and, on the contrary, the bridge pose showed me that my back isn't as stiff as I thought. You're the Master, I thought you knew this by now?" He chuckled.

We continued our training.

Concerning the Basics

The first step in this style is your own. Before unraveling yourself in this art, be conscious of the way their feet hit the ground.

To increase your self-awareness, a fluid plan of strength/endurance training and the basis of meditation will be introduced. This style requires consistent, healthy physical training; no limp body will survive.

Misunderstanding the current elements of your person will make your training lopsided. Many practitioners tend to specialize or generalize in their respective disciplines, with no understanding of their true attitude toward themselves, their fellow humans, and the world around them. Because of this misstep, their footwork and groundwork are flawed.

It is imperative to note that speed of progress is not important. The simple fact that progress is made is enough. Any educator of worth will not penalize their student for "slow progress." As your own teacher, be strict, but do not castigate yourself.

<u>Concerning Thoughts</u>

Create the foundations of your meditation and training. Create a meditation regimen and stick to it. This helps your actions become thoughtless. After much time beginning meditation, your true thoughts, feelings, and beliefs will surface. Do not ignore them.

If the revelation of toxic thoughts is upsetting, be upset. If your beliefs turn out to be shallow, do not desperately make them deeper. If you are feeling many emotions at once, let them overwhelm you.

Bringing all flaws to light and feeling your feelings is imperative for growth. Examine your desires, then relinquish any desire that provides little to no sustenance to your body and mind.

Once you are free from unnecessary and toxic thoughts and beliefs, you may progress.

Such freedom will definitely take time. Take that time to purge yourself.

Concerning Meditation

The foundation of your meditation will start with finding a spot separate from the noise and the clutter of the world. Sit comfortably, breathe and, for one minute, let your thoughts pass by. Whether these thoughts are of your schedule beyond the minute or of something that you recently experienced, let it come to you without force.

As the thought passes by, inhale slowly for five seconds, exhale for five seconds. Once the time is up, slowly recall your thoughts and your feelings, as if explaining them to yourself. Ask yourself the Who, What, Where, When, Why, and How of every thought.

The answers may already be known, but there are moments when thoughts are so quick they are not examined, thus leaving ourselves without proper definition for our actions. Not examining one's thoughts and feelings makes the practitioner limp and useless.

Devoid of anchor
The ebony ship sets sail
Adrift, afloat, peace

Journey's first step made
Fundamental movements learned
Most challenging task

Empty your contents
Except one sip, then fill up
Infinity Cup

Emptying teacup
Tip-toed by sweet turbulence
One piece, still standing

A sinking thought drops
Flowing through body and mind
Sound of inner tide

The world, a teacher
Speaking many simple truths
Hear at your own risk

Acorn, falls from tree
Magpies catch, travel, and drop
Grow up far, child

Two Grapplers embrace
One mind waits, one mind wanders
One Grappler submits

White flower sways left
Seeds glitter across landscape
Blooming with no thought

Sloshy, springtime day
Past dissolves into puddle
Feet plop in the plash

Potential, hidden
With no prying, stays hidden
Critters under stone

Bear at river bends
Pawing through liquid curtain
Sunday Salmon Lunch

Mindlessly Mindful
Flock leaves messy North behind
Mindfully Mindless

Pathway filled by snow
Littered with indented feet
Snow carves a pathway

Steps lie sunken, light
Down the path into the road
Crossing the threshold

Ornamental House
Pictured, revered, and spotted
Sinking foundation

Center your body
Breathe with the wind at your back
Iso, circuit, stretch

THE WHITE CHAPTER

LILLIAN
SNOW WOLF
SINCLAIR

Age: 40

Favorite Music Genre: Psychedelic Funk

Background: After inheriting her family's vast land fortune in Haiti, she used a portion of it as training ground for the other Wolves. When not tending to the farm, she can be found musing on her training in the middle of her property. Music can sometimes be heard emanating from the house.

Snow came into town a couple of months ago for holiday. She took a direct flight from Haiti and stayed with me for a week. During her stay, she insisted on going antique hunting. To her nothing is better finding good deals from the past. I followed, placing a bet with myself that I'd drag her out of five shops this time. Our first stop was a shop called *The Musty Dive,* a pop culture specialty memorabilia. Even with the stuffy scent filling my nostrils, we, surprisingly, unearthed some rare finds. I grabbed a replica medallion from my favorite movie, *The Last Dragon*. It had a dragon serpentine in the middle with the movie name and feature date encircling the dragon. Snow snatched a vinyl featuring music from the prolific Japanese artist, Tsuneo Imahori.

After noticing the particular photograph of the guitarist used as the album cover, the store clerk lectured her on the vinyl. I stood by pretending to look at some bobblehead toys.

He got a few details wrong, like the artist's musical style and the pronunciation of his name. She gave him a look that suggested maybe he should stop to recover. His verbal tirade continued nevertheless. Snow gently, positively, corrected the clerk and added how the artist was influential in a number of anime soundtracks including GunGrave. Her personal favorite. The clerk leaned down from his heightened register perch and asked, 'You know anime is Japanese, right?' His continued, his vernacular elongated and his tone shortened as though she was his student. Snow simply questioned each assertion with the same attitude, not letting any of his "facts" pass by. The clerk revisited his statements each time with a "Well, sure, you're right on that point, but…" only to posit another false claim. Snow just asserted herself, never wavering. After five minutes, the clerk ran out of steam and rung her up.

We walked out with our prizes and got some dumplings. I wore my medallion over my shirt, and she smuggled her stash of records under the table. She munched on a dumpling, saying, "I don't know what that guy's problem was. He was so into arguing, as if his life depended on being right. If his life truly depended on it, he could've checked his phone."

She took another bite.

Begin the process of freshness, untethering your mind from pain and suffering. Now the 4 tenets, or legs, can begin. They are Adaptability, Awareness, Emotions, and Survival.

After realizing self-delusions and your own unconscious thoughts, the first step is to learn detachment. Untether yourself from outer influences, such as others' emotions or unfortunate circumstances. This is when emotional intuition and stability is introduced, and the art of meditation is intensified.

<u>The 4 Tenets</u>

Now is the time to fully examine your current self and ponder on lessons learned. As you come upon a question, realize that your mind may harbor unhelpful solutions, such as spiraling around a single thought without end, or harboring negative thoughts that cause emotional self-harm. Do away with them. How can constant self-nagging bring about positive change?

ADAPTABILITY

One's movement should be supple and limber. When hiking through the forest, bumps, rocks, and crags are abundant. A Wolf moves subtly through such terrains by molding her paws with the ground beneath.

Do not seek a smooth path. There will be none. Energy is wasted when continuously searching for a 'better' path. A good path is one that leads you to your destination with minimal worry and danger.

Take note of the situations you venture into or are brought upon you. What was the most optimal path, and which path did you choose?

AWARENESS
Concerning Self
Understand your own emotional threshold. How does the body react to hate, fear, happiness, or joy? How are your thoughts affected by those emotions? Our emotions drive our thoughts and our thoughts fuel our emotions. Take note of your thoughts and your emotions as you find your answers. Experiment and investigate this thoroughly.

Concerning Others
Be wary of others' stances as they converse, as they fight, and even during peacetimes. Any incident can spurn the best and worst from others. A Wolf moves in accordance with her understanding of the other, whether enemy or friend.

Treading sloppily while a friend is agitated or uneasy results in confusion and can lead to petty quarreling. With friends and allies, carelessness facilitates misunderstanding. Be mindful of your words and movements. Same for an enemy. Carelessness reveals sets up disaster.

If you wish to destabilize your enemy from their center, have your movements be deliberately sloppy. This requires forethought and insight into their mindset. This is useful for battle.

Treading too carefully while an inviting friend is needlessly sensitive. Be patient and kind, open up as well. For an enemy that is dispatched, this movement is overly paranoid. Judge the situation accordingly. Knowing who is friend or foe will help inform your movement.

Understanding the other's true intent helps your movement become more efficient. Once their stance is known, your own stance can be solidified or loosened.

Concerning Surroundings

How does the stream move? Does the wind push against your chest or back? Is the ground weak as you walk? Are others present? Do they notice you? What paths take you to your target? Be present and mindful as you take notice.

EMOTIONS

Concerning Ferocity & Calmness

There is no question that battles involve emotion, sometimes more so than logic. Which emotions and their consequences should be used then? Whichever are effective and prove true to the fighter.

Ferocity is the emotion that excites the muscles and springs the body into action, unlike Satisfaction or Sorrow. Yet using this emotion without discipline, a Wolf becomes frenzied and forgets her strategy.

At this point, calmness is introduced. Retrieving yourself from the brink can be done with reminders of your humanity. Meditate on your humanity and validity by focusing on your positive traits and what you bring to the world, and yourself.

SURVIVAL

To survive, a balanced mind and body is needed. An erratic mind will miss traps and obstacles; a slow mind will fail to keep up with the world. A weak body will not weather the storm. A body whose only attribute is strength will succeed in few things, and fail in many others.

Keep in mind all successes and deficiencies to continually develop the Self.

<u>Concerning Meditation</u>

At this stage, try to increase your meditation ritual by two minutes, continuing the same breathing exercises as before.

While breathing, picture yourself in the center of a room. In front of you is a door, unlocked. After ten seconds, the last person who vexed you walks through. The same vicious words are said and the same actions dealt. As the vitriol is spread, see through their words. Find their intent. Do not be bothered. Is their anger a result of a misdeed, or is it misplaced? Are they communicating discomfort in the only language they know how? See through their emotion and find the source of the problem. Once found, dismiss that person with grace.

Enter the next person. This is the last person who filled you with sorrow. Accept the sadness that comes with their words, and move through it as gently as moving through a pool of water. With or without words, comfort yourself and the other. Be truthful in your speech and actions. Once you have moved through the sorrow, bid that person farewell.

As more people with their own emotion come through, breathe throughout and do not dwell. Once a situation is done, it is done. For people who use their emotion needlessly, set a boundary and

calm them. For those who are vulnerable and open,
treat them well, as you would your best self.

No time for quarrels
Fraught by foes, inner voices
Don't debate bullies

White snow, golden sun
Flowers bloom, flowers suffer
All flowers act out

A path, smooth and paved
Fun for detours and the sights
Brief, simple respite

Wind waltzes with hands
Air cha·chas between fingers
Always a duet

Sparkling Energy
Conforming to the pathway
Flowing to the brim

Noting outer-concern
Start meditative action
Start inner-concern

Hot air vibrating
Uneasy, harried, annoyed
Such refreshing steam

So sensational
Each thin hair electrified
On the tip, a storm

Dirt, rock, and sand mix
Temperaments merging, coolly
Thriving plant garden

On Adaptation
Strife and grief berth new movement
Births insular minds

The air can whip you
No abandon, no remorse
For it is relaxed

THE RED CHAPTER

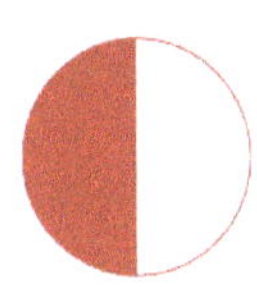

VIRGINIA WOLF

Age: 30

Favorite Treat: Belgian Waffles

Background: After completing her Brazilian Jiu Jitsu training, she traveled to learn Wolf Style. Her tenacity and raw power come from her unbridled enthusiasm. She honed her skill through self-understanding, focusing on the line between calmness and fury.

Virginia voraciously ate through her walnut and apricot salad, as I munched through a garden salad wrap. She taught her Brazilian Jiu-jitsu class not too long ago, and her appetite fully felt the workout. She brought me along as a surprise to her students and to demonstrate how Wolf Style can supplement other martial styles, and so she could boast that she knew the Number One Fighter in the World. Her young students implored us to spar, but, ever the thoughtful instructor, Virginia promised an exhibition only after everyone went through their drills perfectly. I could feel the intensity from each student. The way each pair would circle the area, size each other up, and strike made me hope Virginia would keep her promise.

After a good 25 minutes, she ordered the class to stop and sit against the wall. Virginia removed her Gi jacket, then instructed one of her students to put five minutes on the clock: "You're going to witness a fight between two masters. Perk up your ears and keep your eyes peeled."

There was no circling. We took our stances, bent our knees slightly, and stilled ourselves, trying to find the perfect moment to strike. 30 seconds passed. The students didn't dare blink. I inhaled softly, then charged. Her reaction time was magnificent. Her strikes were fierce. Each attempted hold became faster and more precise than the last. Virginia's fighting zeal became more pronounced with each move. That was something I always admired about her. The one Wolf as quick with an outburst as she is with a tender voice. She used her emotions, specifically anger, as a sort of multiplier for her movements. Incensed yet calm. I dug deep to keep up and defend. The clock chimed and we both stopped mid-charge. Virginia, panting, turned to her students and commanded them to take what they just saw to heart and work to get to our level.

I asked her once where her power came from. "It's sort of from a place of hurt," she said. "I saw my friend get hit by a car at a young age. I ran out

to try and tackle him out of the way, but I guess I
was so scared of getting hit myself, I hesitated to
go at full speed.

This energy comes from when I didn't give
one-hundred percent to help that person.
Watching the life being stolen from him convinced
me that holding back hurts more than one person.
If I can command myself to go one-hundred
percent, then maybe that scene won't play out for
someone else."

<u>Rabid Wolf Style</u>

Now, we shall focus on emotional intuition and the state of fire and transformation. Energy comes from emotion in all of its forms: Rage, calmness, hope, envy, compassion, etc., can all be called upon when one understands their emotional states.

There is a style that capitalizes on one's frenzied state: Rabid Wolf Style. The style provides an unrelenting force, using wildness as an enhancer of strength, speed, and endurance. Like a coiled snake within, the fury should spur the body to spring up and unleash itself. Proper meditation awakens this skill.

A Wolf with self-control can return from this state without harm to her psyche. Practice comes in the form of mastering stillness and understanding the self. Be cautious of practitioners who only focus on the rage aspect, but do not teach stillness. Both loud and quiet moments need full attention in a fight.

True mastery involves feeling the anger, knowing its origin, and commanding the anger to complement your power.

The first step is easy; the second and last steps require mental calmness so the fighter will not mindlessly punch and kick in battle, ripping themselves apart.

Consistent meditation will help find Serenity.

<u>Concerning Meditation</u>

Continue on your meditation from before. Increase the duration by another minute, if you can. When ready, focus on your anger. Where does it come from? When its origin is known, experiment in harnessing and expressing it. Make sure to express your anger at the true intended target. Lashing out at any anyone or thing is sign of thoughtlessness.

That is strictly prohibited.

Frozen in space-time
A rollicking fire seethes
Momentary flash

Young ones, so playful
Tumbleweeds rolling around
Hearty tornadoes

Nestled at the base
Cradling budding passion
Fuel for being

Stems spreading beneath
Holding firmly to the mud
A hundred-year home

Natural Pleasure
A gut reaction expelled
Joyful fulfillment

One hundred punches
Thoughts splintering from each blow
Punches takes over

Guttural microbes
Chanting in great unison
Singular voices

Mind hurried, rattled
Chanting different songs at once
Step back, silence it

When the soul is fixed
The thinking mind is resolved
Such satisfaction

THE
MOUNTAIN
CHAPTER

FRANCOIS
STONE WOLF
MONTAGNARD

Age: 50

Favorite Hangout Spot: Near the lighthouse by the beach

Background: A nomad who sought new forms of expression through martial arts. He doesn't like crowds and mostly speaks in short sentences, but is willing to teach his survival skills to fellow practitioners.

I bumped into Stone at the most unexpected place, the Internet café. I scanned him up and down to make sure I wasn't looking at a mirage. But it was him, in the flesh! He sat at a monitor with a large hiking bag next to the table, single-finger typing, the same way my grandparents would. After he graduated to Master Wolf, he said he needed to travel some more for "better clarity." Of what, I don't know. That was four years ago.

Without turning, he greeted my reflection in the screen. He was writing an email to Grey. Apparently, they corresponded to each other regularly. He finished the email and we walked outside, catching up on each other's lives. He trained and competed in various small tournaments around the U.S., placing first in all of them, using the prize money to pay for meals and camping gear. He camped along the trails outside of towns to focus on meditation and bird watching.

I talked about my success in finally becoming a magazine journalist for 5-7-5 magazine and getting a publishing deal with them. He smiled, and congratulated me on the new position. I was happy with it, but was still troubled. I explained how the writing world was different than expected. Article deadlines were harsh, my publisher had high expectations of my work, the marketing meetings were spoken in an alien language, and there's a lot of promises being made of my writing going far, but no guarantee. Not to mention travelling for work interfered with training. It all left me a bit anxious and exhausted. What's worse, I'd been stuck on the same haiku for a week with the book deadline coming up. Plus, the low wage wasn't helping.

Stone absorbed my troubles. I apologized for taking up so much space. After a moment of silence, he told me a story about one of the tournaments he was in. "I noticed in every match that both fighters would step towards each other and practically press their faces together, grimacing along the way. Everyone did this. I suppose the first thing they wanted to pay attention to were the pores on their opponent's face and show how intimidating they could be.I managed to stay away from my opponents so I wouldn't miss the limp from a bad knee, or the fearful shakes from anxiety.

Don't step too close to the problem, Yendor. You might miss an opportunity to get back on track and be a better writer." He set his hiking pack down and rifled through the side pocket, producing a checkbook. He scribbled what looked like $2,000. "Here, for the apartment. I don't really need much of my winnings. It was serendipitous that we ran into each other today."

<u>Expression</u>

With emotional intuition and a better sense of self, practicing self-expression is the next step on your journey. This starts with identifying your needs. One such need can be from deprivation, e.g. a need for food, and that self-expression can come in the form of cooking a meal for one's self or finding a meal in a vast culinary landscape. Another may be a need for growth, such as socialization. Expression can be in the form of creating quality time with a large social gathering, or a single person. It is all up to the practitioner.

Personally, I found my own fulfillment involved surviving in nature. Determining one's state in the world via communing and enduring the elements built a sense of self-trust that few other activities provided. However, not every practitioner is the same. Survival in our modern times can encompass any activity. In order to find your form, find the activity that assists with self-actualization.

Beware of activities that feed on cravings. Anything that forms an addiction is not a worthwhile activity. Imbibing alcohol or drugs, for example, does not help with self-expression. Typically, it is the social bonding that surrounds the activity that is important.

Challenge yourself to be honest and responsible in your search for self-expression. This involves vulnerability. It will not be easy, but with time and meditation, you will be more aligned with your self.

As always, the above is ultimately up to the practitioner.

<u>Concerning Meditation</u>

Now, take your meditation outside of your mind into the world. Find one activity that you wish to do and practice it for one month. Each day, do at least one thing that will help progress your practice, whether it be writing one line of poetry or a simple study of what ingredients can spice up a stew. This will build a hearty base for your skill. Next, add your own personality to it. This can only be done by being vulnerable and giving yourself the space to move about without interruption.

Afterward, share said skill with those around you. A weakness of meditation is a constant focus on the self to the point of negative self-centeredness. Use this time to exercise vulnerable communication and sharing with those around you. This will also provide a gateway to practice/employ empathy.

Mastering the skill is not the immediate goal; deepening your understanding of yourself, and your relation to others, is.

Forest leaves rustle
Bobbing, bouncing with the wind
On an unknown course

Strikes collide CRACK BOOM
Nothing ornate about it
Gracefully rhythmic

Dull, stagnant rivers
Cannot appease the drinker
Flow to satisfy

To hear your heart's beat
Open your throat, free your song
A chipper warble

The crimson flower
Diet of air and water
Exquisite Banquet

Melodies ringing
Perky light exudes outward
A Choir practice

Vines wrap around stone
Water races through the stream
Take care of your shape

THE
LUNAR
CHAPTER

KIM
SON WOLF
YUNG-LI

Age: 22

Favorite Type of Weather: Sunny with a chance of clouds

Background: A practitioner of Kung Fu and other Chinese arts, he delved into Buddhism before learning Wolf Style. His previous training granted him enlightenment, leaving him empty. He is always kind and understanding.

I never pegged Son as an axe thrower but there we were, sitting at a bar chatting with other axe- league members about throwing technique, and what recipes work best with pesto. Son deftly maneuvered between each group, his social enthusiasm guiding him. I hung back a bit, listening to the conversations.
After a few moments, Son and another were called up for a match. The games were played in pairs, with both throwers competing for points by hitting the target with their axes. The inside of three concentric rings represented one of three possible scores: the first inner ring was one point, the second inner ring was three points, and a bullseye was worth five points.

Son and his opponent geared up for the first of five throws. Both threw a bullseye. His opponent shifted his footing while Son kept still, noticing a ladybug crawling up his arm. When the ref called for the next throw, Son set the ladybug on his shoulder and threw without hesitation. Another bullseye. His opponent only got three points.

Keeping the ladybug on his shoulder, Son's third and fourth throws never wavered: two more bullseyes. His opponent, uneven in his movements, shifted his stance again, raised his hand two inches higher and threw. Another three points for both throws. On their final throw, another twin bullseye. With a score of $25 - 19$, the game went to Son. They shook hands and went back to the group.

After all the matches finished, we walked toward the train station, the ladybug still on his shoulder. I asked him how he got into the sport. He was never much for competitions. He shrugged. "It seemed like fun." I was shocked at how good he was at the game. "I'm only good because I found my footing. The other players are really good too, but they think too deeply about their technique. I step up, breathe, throw, and think of nothing else. If the other guy didn't change his footing so much, we would've tied."

<u>Emptiness</u>

This chapter concerns itself with emptiness. The student should stand on the thin line of beginning and ending during their meditations. Moreover, any student should approach the act of emptiness with no concern for what has already happened. Throughout training, only the essentials should be in place. All cumbersome facets of one's personality are either forsaken or refined.

It should be no surprise that a new being has formed from the physical, mental and emotional exercises of the prior meditations. Seeking balance, managing concerns, perfecting control, and realizing what true survival means has a way of stripping away excess.

Examine this new self. Embrace, understand, and refine this being, as she is still flawed. To further refine, return to the beginning and start the process of emptying yourself of redundancy.

Chaotic bedroom
No space for joy or footsteps
Only restless nights

Rain dropping wet beats
Waves from sunrise to sunset
Realize groove pattern

In cocoon asleep
Calm breaths wash away the past
The body empty

Haibun

The day I became a master, I felt uneasy during celebration. Old Grey, Virginia, Snow, Stone, and Son were there, Snow and Stone still in the process of going through their cycle. Each of them were congratulating me on conquering many of years physical training and meditation. My teacher proudly gave me a hug, but sensed I wasn't enjoying myself.

After the festivities, we skipped the day's training session and went fishing. There was a large pond near Snow's farm that we all visited to be alone with our thoughts. Now was the time.

I told my teacher I didn't feel I accomplished what I needed to accomplish. I was no more enlightened than when I started. Stronger, yes, but I didn't know what else was missing.

My teacher told me this: "As a beginner, I saw myself as simply a man who wanted to learn martial arts. As I delved deeper into it, I became a student studying the minutiae of every punch, kick, and throw. Now, as a master myself, I see myself as a man who wants to learn martial arts. You don't feel different because maybe you didn't need to be different, at the core. You are now a refined young man. Keep sharpening yourself and you'll be fine."

Baby laughs with glee
Grass blades tickling his feet
Adult laughs with glee